Drawing and Learning About Jungle Animals

Using Shapes and Lines

written and illustrated by
Amy Bailey Muehlenhardt

Thanks to our advisers for their expertise, research, and advice:

Linda Frichtel, Design Adjunct Faculty, MCAD
Minneapolis, Minnesota

Susan Kesselring, M.A., Literacy Educator
Rosemount–Apple Valley–Eagan (Minnesota) School District

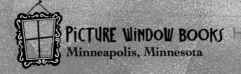

PICTURE WINDOW BOOKS
Minneapolis, Minnesota

Amy Bailey Muehlenhardt
grew up in Fergus Falls, Minnesota,
and attended Minnesota State
University in Moorhead. She holds
a Bachelor of Science degree in
Graphic Design and Art Education.
Before coming to Picture Window
Books, Amy was an elementary art
teacher. She always impressed upon
her students that "everyone is an artist."
Amy lives in Mankato, Minnesota,
with her husband, Brad, and
daughter, Elise.

For Elise Lauren, my new smile.
ABM

Editorial Director: Carol Jones
Managing Editor: Catherine Neitge
Creative Director: Keith Griffin
Editor: Jill Kalz
Editorial Adviser: Bob Temple
Story Consultant: Terry Flaherty
Designer: Jaime Martens
Page Production: Picture Window Books
The illustrations in this book were created with pencil
and colored pencil.

Picture Window Books
5115 Excelsior Boulevard
Suite 232
Minneapolis, MN 55416
1-877-845-8392
www.picturewindowbooks.com

Library of Congress Cataloging-in-Publication Data
Muehlenhardt, Amy Bailey, 1974–
Drawing and learning about jungle animals / written and
illustrated by Amy Bailey Muehlenhardt.
p. cm. — (Sketch it!)
Includes bibliographical references and index.
ISBN 1-4048-1193-1 (hardcover)
1. Jungle animals in art—Juvenile literature. 2. Drawing—
Technique—Juvenile literature. I. Title: Jungle animals. II. Title.
NC783.8.J85M84 2005
743.6—dc22   2005007175

Table of Contents

Everyone Is an Artist

There is no right or wrong way to draw!

With a little patience and some practice, anyone can learn to draw. Did you know every picture begins as a simple shape? If you can draw shapes, you can draw anything.

The Basics of Drawing

line—a long mark made by a pen, a pencil, or another tool

guideline—a line used to help you draw; the guideline will be erased when your drawing is almost complete

shade—to color in with your pencil

value—the lightness or darkness of an object

shape—the form or outline of an object or figure

diagonal—a shape or line that leans to the side

Before you begin, you will need

a pencil,
an eraser,
lots of paper!

Four Tips for Drawing

1. Draw very lightly.
   Try drawing light, medium, and dark lines. The softer you press, the lighter the lines will be.

2. Draw your shapes.
   When you are finished drawing, connect your shapes with a sketch line.

3. Add details.
   Details are small things that make a good picture even better.

4. Color your art.
   Use your colored pencils, crayons, or markers to create backgrounds.

Let's get started!

Simple shapes help you draw.

Practice drawing these shapes before you begin.

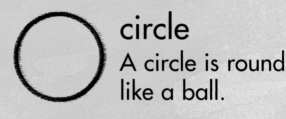 **circle**
A circle is round like a ball.

 **triangle**
A triangle has three sides and three corners.

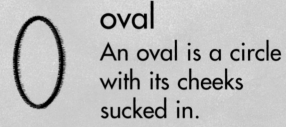 **oval**
An oval is a circle with its cheeks sucked in.

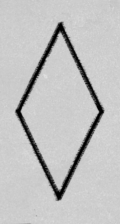 **diamond**
A diamond is two triangles put together.

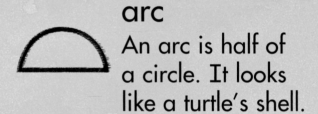 **arc**
An arc is half of a circle. It looks like a turtle's shell.

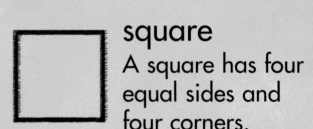 **square**
A square has four equal sides and four corners.

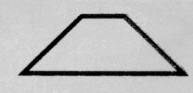 **trapezoid**
A trapezoid has four sides and four corners. Two of its sides are different lengths.

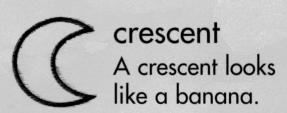 **crescent**
A crescent looks like a banana.

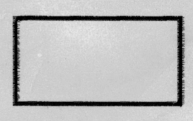 **rectangle**
A rectangle has two long sides, two short sides, and four corners.

You will also use lines when drawing.

Practice drawing these lines.

| vertical
A vertical line stands tall like a tree.

 zigzag
A zigzag line is sharp and pointy.

horizontal
A horizontal line lies down and takes a nap.

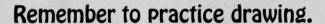 wavy
A wavy line moves up and down like a roller coaster.

diagonal
A diagonal line leans to the side.

Remember to practice drawing.

While using this book, you may want to stop drawing at step five or six. That's great! Everyone is at a different drawing level.

dizzy
A dizzy line spins around and around.

Don't worry if your picture isn't perfect. The important thing is to have fun.

Be creative!

Tree Frog

The tree frog uses the sticky pads on its feet to cling to tree branches. It sits still and waits for a tasty insect to pass. Then it shoots its long tongue out and snatches the bug from the air.

Step 1

Draw an oval for the body. Add a triangle for the head.

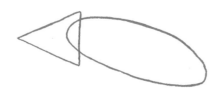

Step 2

Draw a circle and an arc for the two eyes. Add ovals inside the eyes for the pupils.

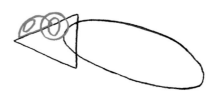

Step 3

Draw three ovals and four rectangles for the legs. Add three circles for the feet. The fourth foot is hiding.

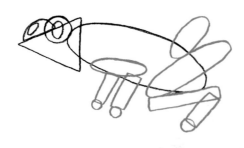

Step 4

Draw nine rectangles and nine circles for the long toes and sticky pads.

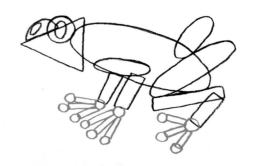

Step 5

Define the tree frog with a sketch line. Add a curved line for the mouth.

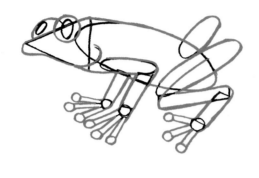

Step 6

Erase the extra lines. Add details such as a leaf for the frog to sit on.

Step 7

Color your animal and add a background.

Praying Mantis

The praying mantis is hard to see because it blends into its surroundings. It looks like a collection of sticks or branches. Strong forelegs and sharp spines help the praying mantis hold its prey.

Step 1

Draw two arcs and an oval for the body. Draw a triangle for the head.

Step 2

Draw eight rectangles for four of the legs. Draw two circles for the eyes.

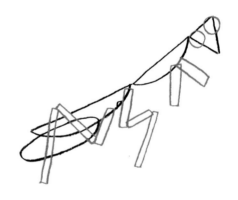

Step 3

Draw four rectangles for two of the legs. Draw one triangle for the back leg and four triangles for the feet.

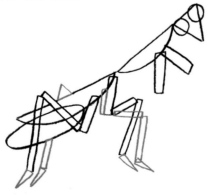

Step 4

Draw two ovals for the front legs. Add two crescents for the claws. Draw two curved lines for the antennae.

Step 5

Define the praying mantis with a sketch line. Add zigzag lines for the front-leg spines. Add curved lines on the abdomen.

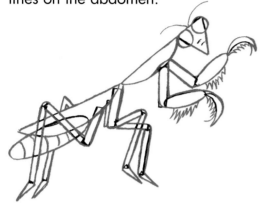

Step 6

Erase the extra lines. Add details such as pupils, and short lines on the face.

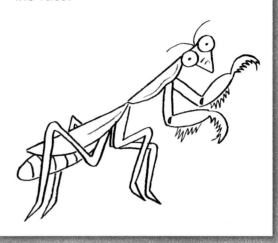

Step 7

Color your animal and add a background.

Jaguar

The jaguar is a large, powerful cat. It hunts in the darkness, sneaking up on its prey and then pouncing. It shows incredible balance as it bounces from rocks to branches in search of food or a place to sleep.

Step 1

Draw an oval and two circles for the body.

Step 2

Draw two circles for the head. Add two arcs for the ears.

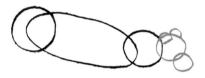

Step 3

Draw six ovals and four rectangles for the legs.

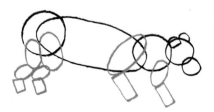

Step 4

Draw four circles for the paws. Add a wavy line for the tail.

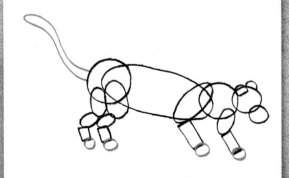

Step 5

Define the jaguar with a sketch line.

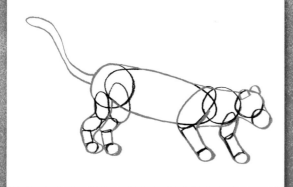

Step 6

Erase the extra lines. Add details such as whiskers, a nose, an eye, and wavy circles for the spots.

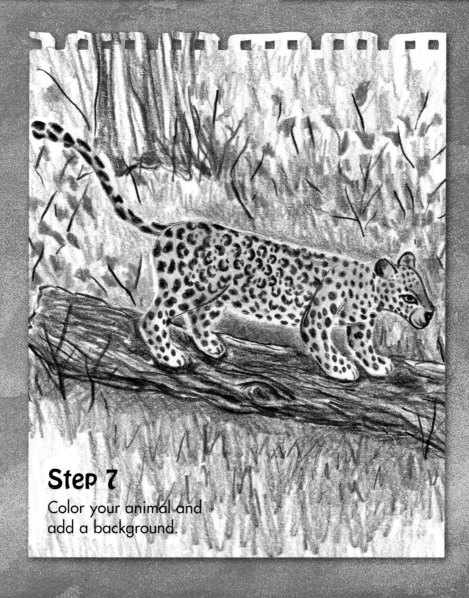

Step 7

Color your animal and add a background.

Tapir

The tapir is a short, round animal that looks like a cross between a tiny horse and a pig. Although its short snout and thick, powerful neck may make it look like a fighter, the tapir isn't fierce. When in danger, it prefers to hide.

Step 1

Draw an oval and an arc for the body. Add a trapezoid for the neck.

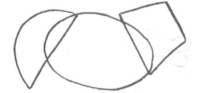

Step 2

Draw one circle for the head and one for the snout. Add an oval for the eye.

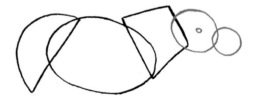

Step 3

Draw two arcs for the ears. Draw four ovals and four rectangles for the legs.

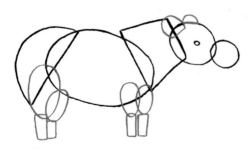

Step 4

Draw four circles for the feet. Add 12 triangles for the claws. Draw two curved lines for the tip of the snout.

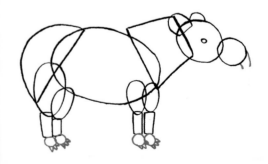

Step 5

Complete the snout with a diagonal line. Create a mouth with a curved line. Add teeth with a diagonal line. Define the tapir with a sketch line.

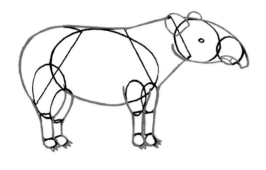

Step 6

Erase the extra lines. Add details such as short, wavy lines on the ears and neck.

Step 7

Color your animal and add a background.

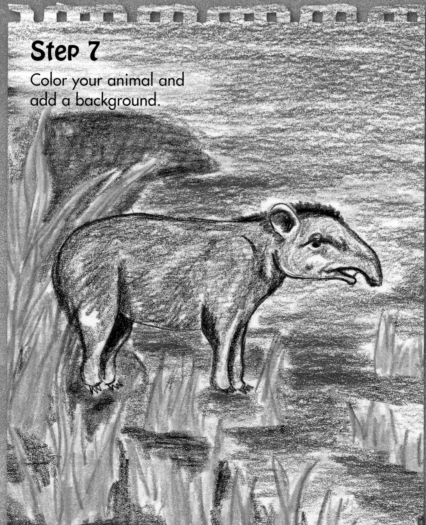

Spider Monkey

The spider monkey uses its long tail and strong hands to grab branches as it swings from tree to tree. It spends its whole life in the treetops, eating fruit, leaves, and seeds.

Step 1

Draw an oval for the body and a circle for the head. Add two circles for the shoulders.

Step 2

Draw three ovals for the legs. Draw four rectangles for the feet.

Step 3

Draw four rectangles and two circles for the arms. Draw two rectangles for the hands. Add a curved line for the tail.

Step 4

Draw four ovals for the eyes. Draw two triangles for the ears and one for the nose. Add a circle for the mouth.

Step 5

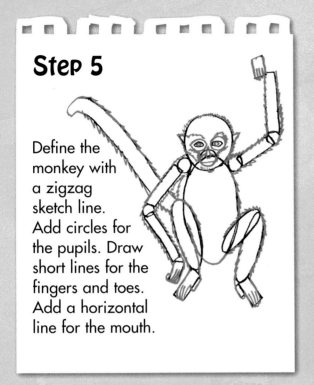

Define the monkey with a zigzag sketch line. Add circles for the pupils. Draw short lines for the fingers and toes. Add a horizontal line for the mouth.

Step 6

Erase the extra lines. Add details such as fur and branches.

Step 7

Color your animal and add a background.

Scarlet Macaw

The scarlet macaw is one of the largest, most colorful parrots in the world. Bright red, yellow, and blue feathers cover its wings and long, slender tail. A curved bill helps the bird crack nuts and tear open fruit.

Step 1

Draw two ovals and a triangle for the wings. Draw an oval for the head.

Step 2

Connect the head to the wings with two curved lines. Add a skinny arc for the body.

Step 3

Draw a triangle and a curved line for the beak. Add a circle for the eye. Draw an oval around the eye.

Step 4

Draw long zigzag lines for the tail feathers. Add four diagonal lines for the tree branch.

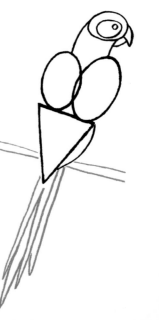

Step 5

Define the parrot with a sketch line. Draw a diagonal line to separate the wings.

Step 6

Erase the extra lines. Add details such as zigzag lines for the feathers.

Step 7

Color your animal and add a background.

Crocodile

The crocodile's eyes peer out from just above the surface of the water. When an animal gets too close, the crocodile's short legs help it explode from the water. It grabs its prey and takes it back into the water for a tasty meal.

Step 1

Draw an oval for the body. Add a trapezoid for the neck.

Step 2

Draw a circle for the head. Add two rectangles and a circle for the snout.

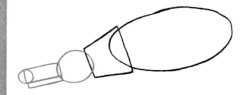

Step 3

Draw six ovals for the legs. Add a crescent for the tail.

Step 4

Draw zigzag lines on each foot for the claws. Add an oval for the eye. The second eye is hiding.

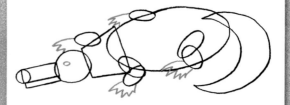

Step 5

Define the crocodile with a sketch line. Draw zigzag lines for the rough skin.

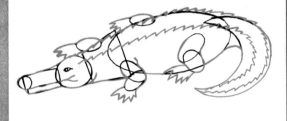

Step 6

Erase the extra lines. Add details such as sharp teeth and a nostril.

Step 7

Color your animal and add a background.

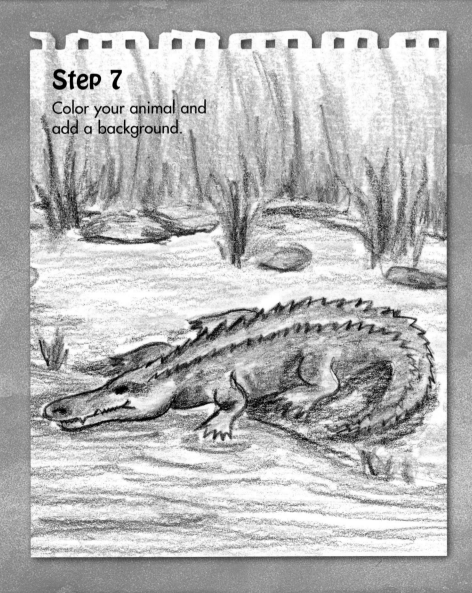

Sloth

The slow-moving sloth spends most of its life in the trees. It hangs upside down by its sharp, hook-like claws. Its fur often has bits of green in it because of the algae growing there. This coloring helps the sloth hide amongst the leaves.

Step 1

Draw an oval for the body. Add a circle for the head.

Step 2

Draw a smaller circle inside the head for the face. Add two circles for the shoulders.

Step 3

Draw four rectangles for the arms. Add two ovals and two rectangles for the legs.

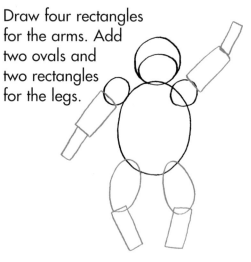

Step 4

Draw two ovals for the eyes. Draw a circle for the nose. Add three crescents and one triangle for the claws.

Step 5

Draw a curved line for the mouth. Define the sloth with a zigzag sketch line.

Step 6

Erase the extra lines. Add details such as pupils, nostrils, fur, and a tree branch.

Step 7

Turn your paper upside down. Color your animal and add a background.

To Learn More

At the Library

Bilgrami, Shaheen. *Jungle Art Show*. New York: Sterling Publishing Co., 2002.

Hart, Christopher. *Kids Draw Animals*. New York: Watson-Guptill Publications, 2003.

Leroux-Hugon, Helene. *I Can Draw Wild Animals*. Milwaukee, Wis.: Gareth Stevens Publishing, 2001.

On the Web

FactHound

FactHound offers a safe, fun way to find Web sites related to this book.

All of the sites on FactHound have been researched by our staff.

http://www.facthound.com

1. Visit the FactHound home page.
2. Enter a search word related to this book, or type in this special code: 1404811931.
3. Click on the FETCH IT button.

Your trusty FactHound will fetch the best sites for you!

Look for all the books in the Sketch It! series:
Drawing and Learning About ...

Bugs	Faces	Monsters
Cars	Fashion	Monster Trucks
Cats	Fish	
Dinosaurs	Horses	
Dogs	Jungle Animals